Acknowledgments

My sincere thanks and appreciation to the following individuals:

For her invaluable help in the preparation of these manuscripts, I thank Paula M. Clark Linkroum. Crystal Osborne for her guidance, talent and design graphics.

For her painstaking editing and advice, I thank my sister, Kim Soibelman.

My gratitude to all Chefs who have contributed their culinary talents throughout the world and have taught me so much. To God, for giving me life, faith and inspiration.

Very special thanks to my family, especially my parents, for their unwavering love and continued support.

To Judy + Norm
"Bon Apetite" Hope you enjoy
from across the Pond.
Love Art + Elsie

The Chefpalate Cookbook

Finding Your Sense of Taste
Cooking With Kalan Soibelman
A Collection of Enchanting Cuisine

By

Kalan Soibelman

This book is a work of fiction. Places, events, and situations in this story are purely fictional. Any resemblance to actual persons, living or dead, is coincidental.

ISBN: 1-4033-7877-0 (e-book)
ISBN: 1-4033-7878-9 (Paperback)
ISBN: 1-4033-8409-6 (Hardcover)

This book is printed on acid free paper.

1st Books - rev. 10/21/02

Dedication

This book is dedicated to my grandfather, Max Soibelman. His good-natured humor has made my life gratifying. He has served as our family patriarch and has been inspirational to all that have passed through his life and he, at 97 years old, continues to inspire me to this day.

Contents

Introduction

In developing The Chefpalate Cookbook, I have combined traditional ingredients, techniques and the sensibilities of modern (or nouvelle) French, Asian and American cuisine.

The recipes in this book grew out of my own experiences at the finest hotels, country clubs and restaurants in which I have worked. I am a classically trained chef and, most importantly, a person who loves food.

I hope that the food you prepare gives you great satisfaction and pleasure, leaving you feeling like you have discovered things you never imagined. After twenty years in the business I am still learning, experimenting and best of all, I am still excited about the never-ending process.

The recipes in this book are meant to show the harmony and marvelous style of good food.

Enjoy,

Kalan Soibelman

To further your sense of taste, visit
www.Chefpalate.com

Appetizers

To begin any great meal you can start with a few of these wonderful, tasty bites. By offering your guests these tantalizing treats, they'll set the tone for your main event or you can use these recipes as an integral part of your main meal.

Avocado Mousse

2 ripe avocados, skinned and pitted
1 T. lemon juice
Salt and pepper to taste

In a food processor or blender, combine avocado and lemon juice. Blend until smooth. Add salt and pepper to taste. Serve immediately.

Serving suggestion: Accompany with the ***rose petal gravlax***.

Beef Tartar

(Serves 2)

½ lb. beef tenderloin
2 egg yolks
2 T. salt
2 T. ground black pepper
2 T. capers, drained
2 T. onions, finely chopped
2 T. parsley, finely chopped
8 anchovy fillets, drained

Fine grind the beef tenderloin. Shape the beef into two mounds and place them in the center of two separate plates. Make a well in the middle of each mound and carefully drop an egg yolk into each.

Serve the salt, black pepper, capers, onions, parsley and anchovies in small, separate saucers. The beef and ingredients are then combined at the table and accompanied by toast points. Serve immediately.

Caviar Crab Cakes

16 oz. crabmeat
½ c. chives
1 tsp. caviar
½ c. mayonnaise
2 T. whole grain mustard
1 tsp. lemon juice
2 eggs
Dry bread crumbs

Preheat oven to 500º.

Combine the ingredients in a bowl and mix. The amount of bread crumbs depends on the wetness of the crabmeat. Mixture should be firm. Oil a baking sheet and shape cakes with a small scoop. Sprinkle with breadcrumbs and oil. Bake until golden brown.

Chili Prawn Cakes

1¼ lbs. raw prawn meat
1 egg
3 T. sweet chili sauce
2 c. fresh bread crumbs
1 bunch cilantro, chopped
1 red bell pepper, cored and diced
1 half of a carrot, diced
Salt and pepper to taste

Place prawn meat, egg, sweet chili sauce and bread crumbs in a food processor. Process until the mixture is combined, but not smooth. Place mixture in a bowl and fold in the cilantro, red bell pepper and carrot. With wet hands, shape the mixture into small cakes.

Heat enough oil in a frying pan over medium - high heat to shallow fry. Add a few prawn cakes at a time and cook for 3 minutes on each side or until golden brown.

Chinese Crisp Noodle

(Serves 4 to 6)

1 lb. fresh Chinese egg noodles
½ c. minced scallions
1 tsp. minced ginger
2 T. soy sauce
4 T. peanut oil

Bring a large pot of water to a boil. Cook the noodles until they are tender, but not mushy. Drain the noodles and toss together with the scallions, ginger, soy sauce and 1 tablespoon of the oil. Pour 2 tablespoons of the oil into a heavy, medium-large skillet, preferably nonstick. Turn the heat to medium-high. When the oil is hot, add the noodle mix, spreading it out evenly and pressing down. Cook for 2 minutes, then turn the heat down to medium-low. Cook until the cake is nicely browned on the bottom, about 10 minutes. Turn carefully and brown the other side. Add the remaining oil to the skillet if necessary. Cut into eighths or quarters and serve.

Corn Cake

2 cobs of corn
1 c. self-rising flour
2 eggs
1 T. baking powder
1 bunch parsley, chopped
Pinch of salt

Place the corn in a saucepan of boiling water and cook until tender. Remove corn kernels from the cob. Place the flour, eggs, baking powder, parsley and salt into a food processor and process until combined. Add the corn and process until corn is roughly chopped. Spread 2-3 tablespoons of mixture onto a hot, greased frying pan and cook for 3 minutes on each side or until golden brown. Keep warm and repeat with remaining mixture.

Serving suggestion: Place a corn cake on each serving plate and top with seared scallops, drizzle with balsamic syrup and top with another corn cake. Serve immediately.

Dill Frittata

4 eggs, lightly beaten
½ c. milk
1/3 c. chopped dill
1/3 c. grated, aged cheddar cheese
Cracked black pepper

Place eggs, milk, dill, cheddar cheese and pepper in a bowl and mix to combine. Pour mixture into a nonstick frying pan and cook on medium heat for 4 minutes or until the Frittata is almost set. Place under a hot grill for 1 minute or until golden brown. Remove from pan and cut into wedges.

Serving suggestion: Top with ***caper aioli***.

Dill Phyllo Cups

4 sheets phyllo dough
4 tsp. melted butter
1 T. chopped dill
Preheat the oven to 375°.

Lightly brush 4-inch tart tins with melted butter. Unroll and lay 1 sheet of phyllo on counter and brush with melted butter. Press phyllo into a tin until it is compacted. Sprinkle with chopped dill. Repeat with the remaining phyllo. Place tins on a baking sheet and bake until golden brown and crisp, about 16 minutes. Allow the edge of the tins to release the cup. Cool on a rack.

Serving suggestion: Fill cups with your favorite mousse, custard or sauce.

Green Scallion Ginger Potato Mash

13 oz. of sweet potatoes, peeled and chopped
2 T. shredded ginger
1 oz. butter
1 T. honey
Milk
1 bunch chopped green scallions (greens only, no white)

Place the sweet potato and ginger in a saucepan of boiling water and cook for 5-7 minutes or until tender, then drain. Mash the sweet potatoes with the butter, honey and enough milk to make it smooth. Fold in green scallions, salt and pepper to taste.

Kaffir Lime and Lemon Chutney

(Makes 3 cups)

6 Kaffir limes
6 lemons
1 c. chopped apples
1 c. brown sugar
¼ tsp. cinnamon
¼ tsp. cardamom
½ T. chopped lemon grass

Peel limes and lemons with vegetable peeler and chop peels in food processor. Remove the white skin from the limes and lemons and discard. Dice limes and lemons, discard the seeds but save the juice. Combine limes, lemons, juice, peels, apples and sugar in nonstick pot and bring to a boil. Add spices and cook until thick.

Kaffir Lime Dip

(Makes 6 cups)

12 Kaffir limes
2 c. mango chunks
1 c. papaya chunks
¼ c. chopped ginger
1 c. sugar

Cut limes in half and remove the seeds. Place in food processor with 1 cup cold water, process with pulse until chopped. Add other ingredients and process until well mixed (a coarse puree). Can be kept refrigerated for up to 1 week. If necessary, dip may be diluted with water.

Province Black Olive Tapenade

(Makes 1 cup)

10 anchovy fillets, packed in salt
2 c. brine black olives, pitted
1 T. capers, drained
1 tsp. Dijon mustard
1 garlic clove, minced
¼ tsp. fresh thyme, chopped
6 T. olive oil

In a food processor, combine the anchovies, olives, capers, mustard, garlic and thyme. Process to form a thick paste. With the processor running, add the oil in a steady stream until it is thoroughly incorporated into the mixture, and then serve.

Kalan Soibelman

Rare Tuna Spring Rolls

1 lb. piece sashimi grade tuna
1 T. wasabi paste
2 T. chopped cilantro
8 spring roll wrappers
Oil for deep-frying

Cut tuna into pieces, approx. 2 cm. wide by 10 cm. long. Spread each piece of tuna very lightly with the wasabi paste. Roll the tuna in the cilantro. Wrap each piece of tuna in a spring roll wrapper, using a little water to seal the ends. Deep-fry the spring rolls in hot oil for 30-45 seconds or until lightly golden brown. Drain on absorbent paper. Cut in half and serve.

Rose Petal Gravlax

1 lb. center-cut fresh salmon fillet, (pin bones removed)
6 T. kosher salt
6 T. sugar
Thin sliced orange rounds
1 T. dried rose petals, ground
1 T. orange liqueur
1 tsp. ground black pepper

Place salmon, skin side down, on a large piece of plastic wrap. Combine the salt and sugar in a bowl. Rub mixture into both sides of the fish. Then top with remaining ingredients. Double-wrap the salmon in plastic wrap. Sandwich it between two small cookie sheets. Place a 4-5 pound weight on top. Refrigerate for 36 hours, turning the package once. To serve, use a slicing knife, cut thin slices about 1/8 inch thick.

Serving suggestion: Top with a dollop of avocado mousse.

Seared Foie Gras

1 fresh duck foie gras, 1 to 1 ½ pounds
Sea salt to taste

Note: Working with chilled foie gras can cause the liver to break. At room temperature, it is malleable and much easier to work with.

Foie gras (duck liver) consists of two lobes, one small and one large. With the tip of a small, sharp knife, carefully remove any trace of green from the surface of the foie gras. With your hands, separate the large lobe from the smaller lobe by gently pulling them apart. Carefully remove the transparent skin surrounding each piece of duck liver. With the tip of the knife, remove and discard the thin red blood vessel that runs lengthwise through the inside of each lobe. With a sharp knife, slice the foie gras diagonally into scallops about ¾ inch thick. Cover with plastic wrap and refrigerate until serving time.

Heat a large, nonstick skillet until it is very hot. Add the foie gras and sear for 30 seconds on each side, turning the pieces carefully with tongs. Transfer the cooked foie gras to a platter covered with paper towels and allow to drain. Sprinkle with sea salt to taste. Transfer to warmed plates.

Serving suggestion: Place a small spoonful of Kaffir lime and lemon chutney alongside the foie gras and serve.

Smoked Trout and Fennel

2 smoked trout
1 c. shaved fennel
1 T. olive oil
1 T. chopped onions
¼ tsp. chopped garlic
¼ tsp. ground nutmeg
1 tsp. kosher salt
1 c. soft cream cheese

Remove skin and debone trout. Flake meat to be sure all bones are removed. Set fish aside. Add fennel to boiling water and quickly blanch, approx. 3 minutes. Drain the fennel then chill in cold water. Sauté onions and garlic in oil until light yellow, add nutmeg, salt and chilled fennel. Cook until thoroughly hot and well mixed. Cool. Add cream cheese and fish.

Serving suggestion: Roll into crepes and finish with caviar.

Sun Dried Tomato Paste Spread

(Makes ½ cup)

10 sun-dried tomatoes
1 garlic clove, minced
6 T. olive oil
Salt to taste
2 tsp. chopped thyme

In food processor, combine all ingredients and process until the paste is lightly coarse, almost chunky.

Serving suggestion: Spread on toast rounds or add to your favorite pasta sauce.

Tuna Tartar

1 lb. fresh tuna fillet
½ oz. olive oil
1 tsp. chopped shallots
1 tsp. chopped capers
1 tsp. chopped parsley
1 tsp. soy sauce
½ tsp. chopped ginger

Dice fish with a sharp knife. (Tuna tail pieces are preferred. Belly and back pieces can be very fatty. Fish should be firm, not squashed or mushy.) Add all remaining ingredients, season with salt to taste.

Salads

These recipes are designed to let you try something new, easy and interesting. Produce is better than ever and there are several varieties of greens to choose from. These salads will shape and trap your favorite vinaigrettes and you're guaranteed a variety of straightforward recipes to start your meal or to serve as the ultimate main course.

Ahi Tuna Mediterranean Vegetable Salad

(Serves 4 to 6)

1 head romaine lettuce, washed and dried
4 tomatoes, quartered
4 hard-boiled eggs, cooled, peeled and quartered
7 oz. fresh ahi tuna, diced
½ c. black olives, Mediterranean style
2 c. blanched green string beans, chilled
2 T. chopped parsley

Line a glass bowl with the lettuce and arrange the tomato quarters, egg quarters, tuna, olives and green beans on top in an attractive pattern. Spoon your favorite vinaigrette over the salad and sprinkle with parsley. Serve immediately.

Artichoke and Goat Cheese Salad

(Serves 4)

3 oz. soft goat cheese
2 T. olive oil
8 artichoke hearts
8 c. mesclun greens

In a food processor, combine the goat cheese and oil. Process until smooth. Spread the cheese mixture into the hollows of the artichoke hearts. Arrange the artichoke hearts side by side on a baking sheet. Place the baking sheet in the oven, about 3 inches from the heat. Broil until the cheese is golden brown and bubbly.

Meanwhile, toss the mesclun greens with your favorite vinaigrette. Arrange the salad on 4 salad plates, place two grilled artichoke hearts along side each portion and serve.

Cannellini Bean Salad

(Serves 6)

1½ c. cannellini beans
2 qt. water
Kosher salt
½ c. olive oil
3 T. lemon juice
1 c. chopped red onion
1 c. vine-ripe tomatoes
4 T. chopped basil
24 medium sized shrimp, peeled and deveined

Place beans in a bowl of water, cover and soak overnight. The following day, drain the beans and place in a saucepan with 2 quarts water. Bring to a boil over medium heat and simmer until tender, about 40 minutes. Add 2 teaspoons of salt during the last 15 minutes of cooking. Remove from heat. Drain beans and transfer to a bowl. Add olive oil, lemon juice, onions, tomatoes and basil. Toss until blended. Season with salt. In a sauté pan, add olive oil and heat over high heat. When hot, add the shrimp and sauté quickly until shrimp is pink and cooked through, approx. 3 - 4 minutes. Spoon beans onto a plate.

Arrange the shrimp around the beans and drizzle with a bit of olive oil. Serve.

Kalan Soibelman

Cherry Tomato, Avocado & Roasted Corn Salad

(Serves 12)

5 ears of corn, shucked
½ c. olive oil
Salt and pepper
3 T. fresh lime juice
2 T. red wine vinegar
1 tsp. sugar
1½ pounds arugula
3 ripe avocados, cut into ½ inch cubes
1 basket red cherry tomatoes, about 30 each
2 medium cucumbers, peeled, seeded and cut into ¼ inch cubes

Preheat the oven to 450°.

On a sheet pan, drizzle the corn with 2 tablespoons of olive oil. Season the ears with salt and pepper and roast for about 25 minutes, until kernels are browned. Let cool. Cut the kernels from the cobs and transfer to a bowl. Place ½ cup corn kernels in a blender. Add the lime juice, red wine vinegar and sugar. With the machine on, add the remaining ½ cup olive oil in a thin stream and blend until emulsified. Scrape the vinaigrette into a bowl and season with salt to taste. In a large bowl, toss the remaining corn kernels with the arugula, avocados, cherry tomatoes and cucumber. Add the vinaigrette and toss well.

Serving suggestion: Mound the salad on a platter, sprinkle with crumbled goat cheese and serve.

Crab Salad with Avocado Cream

(Serves 6)

4 uncooked crabs
3 T. crème fraîche or heavy cream
2 T. lemon juice
2 tsp. finely chopped mint
1 tsp. finely chopped tarragon
Salt
Freshly ground black pepper
2 finely sliced carrots
Mint leaves for garnish

Bring a large pot of water to boil. Add the crabs and cook for 6 minutes, then plunge them into cold water. Remove their flesh and mix with the crème fraîche, lemon juice, chopped mint and tarragon. Season with salt and pepper. Chill.

Avocado Cream

2 lg. avocados
2 T. crème fraîche or heavy cream
Juice of 2 lemons

Blend the avocados with the crème fraîche and half the lemon juice until smooth. Pour the remaining lemon juice on top and chill until ready to serve.

To serve, place a pastry cutter on each plate and spoon in the carrot and crabmeat mixture. Stir the avocado cream until lemon juice is blended, then spoon it onto each salad. Carefully remove the rings. Garnish with the mint leaves.

Cumin Parmesan Crisp Cup

3 c. fresh grated Parmesan cheese
½ tsp. ground cumin

Combine ingredients. Heat an 8-inch nonstick sauté pan over medium heat. Sprinkle about 1 oz. of the cheese mixture evenly over the bottom of the skillet to make a thin pancake. You should not be able to see the bottom of the skillet. The cheese should bubble and melt together. As the edges begin to brown, remove from heat and, with a rubber spatula, gently lift the crisp by the edge and flip. Then melt the other side. The crisp should be golden brown when finished. Slide crisp over an inverted coffee cup and form around the cup. Let cool and remove crisp cup.

Serving suggestion: Fill crisp cup with salad. This makes a spectacular salad or appetizer.

Moroccan Cucumber Salad

(Serves 4)

½ garlic clove, sliced thin, lengthwise
1 shallot, sliced thin, lengthwise
2½ T. fresh lemon juice
1 tsp. kosher salt
1 tsp. sugar
2 T. olive oil
4 English seedless cucumbers
1 lb. pear tomatoes, red and yellow
1 oz. chopped flat-leaf parsley
1 oz. crumbled feta cheese

In a large bowl add garlic, shallots, lemon juice, salt and sugar. Whisk in the olive oil. Peel the cucumbers, slice lengthwise and dice. Add to the bowl. Slice the tomatoes lengthwise and add to the bowl. Add parsley and feta cheese. Chill and serve.

Kalan Soibelman

Seared Quail Over Mesclun Greens

(Serves 4)

8 quail
2 chopped garlic cloves
1 tsp. olive oil
Kosher salt
2 tsp. balsamic vinegar
2 tsp. red wine vinegar
2 T. olive oil
8 c. mesclun salad greens

Rub the quail lightly with olive oil, garlic and salt. Set aside. In a small bowl, combine the balsamic and red wine vinegar and olive oil. Add salt to taste. Place greens in a bowl and drizzle with the vinegar and oil mixture. Arrange the greens on a plate. Heat a nonstick skillet over high heat. Add quail, skin side down. Cook for 1 minute, turn over and cook for 1 minute more. Make sure quail is cooked through. Remove quail and cut in half. Place over greens and serve.

Seasonal Fruits and Peppery Greens

(Serves 4)

12 oz. watercress, radicchio and Belgian endive, trimmed and cleaned
1 red pear, peeled, cored and sliced
4 figs, cut into quarters
1 blood orange, peeled and sectioned
1 tangerine, peeled and sectioned
4 kumquats, sliced crosswise into very thin slices

Put the greens in a large bowl and scatter the fruit over them.

Serving suggestion: For a wonderful finish to this salad, top with citrus vinaigrette and nuts.

Sesame Salad with Scallops

(Serves 4)

2 lbs. sea scallops
¼ c. soy sauce
¼ c. rice wine
2 T. peanut butter
1 T. sesame oil
¼ tsp. crushed red pepper flakes
1 T. honey
1 T. peeled and chopped ginger
8 c. mesclun salad greens
1 T. toasted sesame seeds

Prepare a large, nonstick skillet over high heat. When the skillet starts to smoke, add the scallops. Brown the scallops, about 1 minute each side. Combine the soy sauce, rice wine, peanut butter, sesame oil, red pepper flakes, honey, and ginger in a blender and puree until smooth. Divide the greens among four plates. Top with scallops and drizzle with dressing. Sprinkle with sesame seeds and serve.

Shredded Raw Crunchy Vegetable Salad

(Serves 4)

4 oz. celery root, julienne or shredded
4 oz. parsnips, julienne or shredded
4 oz. fennel, julienne or shredded
4 oz. carrots, julienne or shredded
4 oz. Chinese cabbage, julienne or shredded
4 oz. red bell pepper, julienne or shredded
Salt and pepper
1 tsp. grated lemon zest
1 tsp. chopped tarragon

In a large bowl, toss the vegetables together with salt and pepper to taste. Prepare salad on plates, top with lemon zest and tarragon.

Serving suggestion: Cider or lemon vinaigrette goes well with this salad.

Sweet Earthy Beet Salad

(Serves 4)

1 lb. baby beets, yellow and red rosy
1 T. balsamic vinegar
1 T. red wine vinegar
1 tsp. lemon juice
Kosher salt to taste
1½ T. of walnut oil
8 oz. Belgian endive, mache and watercress
1 pear, peeled, cored and diced
1 T. chopped walnuts
Preheat oven to 450°.

Cut stems and roots off beats and peel skin. Place beets in a small roasting pan with approx. 1/8-inch water. Cover and roast for 30 minutes, until they are tender. Let beets cool and slice into half moons. In a medium bowl, add beets, balsamic vinegar, red wine vinegar, lemon juice and salt. Toss until blended. Add walnut oil and continue to toss until blended. Place a mound of greens on each plate. Place the beet mixture on top. Garnish with the pear and walnuts.

Sweet Ginger Vinaigrette

(Makes ½ cup)

1/3 c. corn, peanut or canola oil
3 T. fresh ginger, grated and peeled
2 T. plus 1 tsp. balsamic vinegar
1 T. sugar

Combine the ginger, balsamic vinegar and sugar in a bowl. Slowly stir in the oil with a whisk. Do not beat. Serve with salad greens.

(Don't worry if the vinaigrette separates. When tossed with salad greens, all the components will coat the greens even if the vinaigrette has not thoroughly emulsified.)

Tuna Carpaccio

(Serves 4)

4 slices fresh ahi tuna
½ c. olive oil
¼ c. lemon juice
1 T. brandy
Salt to taste
2 bunches watercress
2 T. chopped chives

Place each slice of tuna between 2 sheets of oiled parchment paper and pound gently. Refrigerate, still in the paper, until needed. In a bowl, whisk together olive oil, lemon juice and brandy. Salt to taste. Toss watercress with vinaigrette. Arrange the greens on a plate. Peel away paper from the tuna and place on top of the greens. Drizzle the remaining vinaigrette on top. Sprinkle with the chopped chives and serve.

Wild Mushroom Salad

(Serves 4)

12 oz. mix of chanterelle and sliced shiitake mushrooms
2 T. chopped shallots
2 chopped garlic cloves
1 T. chopped thyme
Kosher salt
1/3 c. red wine vinegar
1 T. olive oil
1 T. balsamic vinegar
6 c. mesclun greens

In a sauté pan, over medium heat, add olive oil. When oil is hot, add mushrooms, shallots and garlic. Sauté until tender and golden brown. Add thyme and salt to taste. Set aside to cool. In a small bowl, combine 1 teaspoon of olive oil, red wine vinegar and balsamic vinegar. Set aside. Reheat mushrooms in pan and add dressing. Cook until mushrooms are warm. Spoon mushrooms and juices over mesclun greens. Sprinkle with herbs and serve immediately.

Soups

It seems impossible to find someone who doesn't like soup and that's wonderful since soups are not only hearty, but also economical. These recipes combine a variety of different ingredients, which will reveal the secret to fine velvety soups. You'll find creative soup recipes to cool you in the summer, warm you up in the winter or to enjoy any time of the year.

Curry Cucumber Soup

(Serves 4)

7 English seedless cucumbers, peeled and chopped
¼ c. fresh lime juice
1 tsp. kosher salt
1 tsp. cardamon
2 T. white wine vinegar
1 tsp. curry powder
1 tsp. cayenne pepper
1 c. plain yogurt

Combine cucumber, lime juice, salt, cardamon, wine vinegar, curry powder and cayenne pepper. Puree the mixture in a blender. Pass through a fine strainer into a large bowl and whisk in the yogurt. Adjust the seasoning with salt. Serve the soup in individual bowls.

Serving suggestion: *Garnish with fresh dill sprig.*

Ginger Crab Soup

(Serves 6)

¾ lb. crabmeat
1 Poblano chili, peeled, seeded and chopped
3 T. olive oil
1 garlic clove, chopped
1 T. finely chopped onion
2 T. fresh ginger juice or finely chopped fresh ginger
1 tsp. saffron
4 c. heavy cream
Salt to taste

Heat the oil in a large heavy-bottomed saucepan over medium heat. Add the garlic, pepper and onion. Sauté for about 3 minutes. Add the ginger juice or fresh chopped ginger. Stir well. Add the crabmeat and bring to a simmer. Stir in saffron and cream. Lower the heat and adjust seasoning with salt to taste. Garnish with fresh crabmeat and serve.

Green Pea and Leek Soup

(Serves 6)

1 small head of lettuce, shredded
2 c. shelled fresh green peas
1 c. water
1 c. chopped leeks (green part only)
2 T. butter
2 tsp. chopped chervil
1 tsp. sugar
1 tsp. salt
2 c. chicken stock

Combine lettuce, peas, water, leeks, butter, chervil, sugar and salt in a heavy saucepan. Over medium-high heat, bring to a boil and cook until peas are tender. Reserve 3 tablespoons of peas for garnish. Pour remaining mixture through a sieve. Return sieve mixture (solids) to the pan. Reheat with 2 cups chicken stock. Garnish with reserved, cooked peas and serve.

Kalan Soibelman

Kalan's Clamy Chowder

(Serves 12)

This is a large amount of Clam Chowder, great for parties.
Prep time is 45 minutes. Cook time is 1 hour 30 minutes.

1 qt. shucked clams, with liquid
1 c. butter
2 c. onion, finely chopped
1½ c. carrots, diced
2 c. celery, chopped
1½ c. corn, fresh
1½ c. all-purpose flour
6 - 8 oz. jars of clam juice
5 c. peeled purple potatoes
3 c. chopped cured sausage
2 qt. half and half
1 1/2 tsp. salt
1/2 tsp. freshly ground black pepper
2 T. red wine vinegar
2 T. chopped tarragon

Melt butter in a large kettle or stockpot, over medium heat. Add onions, carrots, celery and corn. Sauté until tender. Stir in flour and cook over low heat, stirring frequently, 4 to 6 minutes. Set aside to cool. In a separate pot, bring clams and clam juice to a boil. Reduce heat and simmer for 15 minutes. In a small saucepan, cover peeled purple potatoes with water. Bring to a boil and cook until potatoes are tender, about 20 minutes. Drain and set aside. Slowly pour hot clam stock into butter-flour mixture while stirring constantly. Continue stirring and slowly bring to a boil. Reduce heat and add cooked potatoes and sausage. Mix in half and half, salt, pepper, red wine vinegar and chopped tarragon. Heat through but do not boil.

Serving suggestion: Serve with hard crust bread or oyster crackers.

Rock Crab Soup

(Serves 6)

3 T. olive oil
2 leeks, rinsed and finely chopped
1 bulb fennel, finely chopped
Kosher salt
2 lbs. live rock crab
3 fresh tomatoes, cored and chopped
½ c. white wine
20 qt. hot water
Sprigs of parsley, bay leaves and thyme
1/8 tsp. saffron

In a 6-quart stockpot, combine the oil, leeks, fennel and a pinch of salt. Sweat cook, covered, over low heat until soft. Stirring from time to time. Increase the heat to high and add crabs. Cover and cook until crabs are colored. Then add tomatoes, wine, hot water and herbs. Season to taste with salt. Bring to rapid boil for 20 minutes. Remove the pot from the heat and strain the mixture through a fine sieve. Return the liquid to the pot and place over high heat. Taste for seasoning and add the saffron. Taste again for seasoning. Serve the broth hot.

Sweet Corn Soup

(Serves 6)

4 c. sweet yellow corn kernels, fresh
1 c. hot chicken stock
4 T. butter
3½ c. milk
½ tsp. salt or to taste
½ tsp. dry chili flakes

Blend the corn in the hot chicken stock at high speed until you have a smooth puree. Put the puree through a food mill or a coarse strainer. Melt the butter in a large saucepan but do not let it get too hot. Add the corn puree and let it cook over medium heat for about 5 minutes, stirring constantly. Add the milk and bring it to a boil. Lower the heat and let the soup simmer. Add the Chile flakes and salt to taste.

Serving suggestions: Serve soup with a garnish of fresh corn kernels and chopped tarragon.

Tomato Gazpacho

(Serves 6-8)

3 Roma tomatoes, diced
2 red bell peppers, cured, seeded and diced
1 English seedless cucumber, diced
1 red onion, diced
2 garlic cloves, chopped
¼ c. red wine vinegar
Salt to taste
2 c. tomato juice
Sour cream, for garnish
Finely chopped chives, for garnish

In a medium bowl, mix together the tomatoes, peppers, cucumber and onions. Add the garlic and red wine vinegar. Cover and marinate in the refrigerator for 4 hours. Place the mixture in a blender, puree it, and then strain it into a clean bowl. Add salt. If the mixture is too thick, it can be diluted with the tomato juice. Serve the soup in a martini glass, garnish with sour cream and chopped chives.

Truffle Puree of Carrot Soup

(Serves 4-6)

2 T. butter
¾ c. chopped onions
3 c. chopped carrots
1 qt. chicken stock
2 tsp. tomato paste
2 T. white raw rice
Salt to taste
White pepper to taste
½ c. heavy cream
½ tsp. truffle oil
1 T. soft butter
12 carrot curls

In a heavy 4-quart saucepan, melt the butter over moderate heat. Add onions and cook, stirring occasionally, for 5 minutes or until they are soft, but not browned. Add the carrots, chicken stock, tomato paste, and rice. Simmer gently, uncovered, for 30 minutes. Puree the soup through a food mill into a saucepan. Season it with salt and white pepper. Stir in cream and truffle oil. Return the soup to low heat and bring it to a simmer. Remove the pan from the heat and stir in the tablespoon of soft butter. To serve, ladle the soup into individual soup bowls.

Sauces

The sauces in this book include a broad range of techniques and ingredients from around the world. A sauce can be any liquid such as a vinaigrette, chutney or flavored oil. Serving a sauce gives your meal that extra touch and can transform your dish into a gourmet meal.

Asian Veal or Beef Stock

(Serves 2 cups)

3 lbs. Veal or beef bones
1 lb. button mushrooms
½ tsp. kosher salt
Fresh black pepper
2 T. chopped parsley
2 halved shallots
2 halved garlic clove
1 chopped ginger
2 tsp. low sodium soy sauce, to taste
1 c. tomato paste

Trim the skin and fat from the bones. In a heavy stockpot, place the bones in cold water and cover by at least 2 inches. Bring to a gentle simmer over medium heat. Skim and remove the film that rises to the surface. As the bones simmer, add cold water to replace the water that has evaporated and continue skimming until broth is clear. Add the remaining ingredients and return the liquid to a gentle simmer. Continue to simmer for 4 hours. Pour broth in a colander over a large bowl and discard the solids. Chill the liquid. Once chilled, spoon off all traces of fat.

Caper Aioli

2 egg yolks
½ tsp. chopped garlic
½ tsp. lemon juice
1 T. capers, drained
Pepper to taste
Extra-virgin olive oil

Combine the yolks, garlic, and lemon juice in a food processor until mixture has developed into a slight foam. Continue to process and gradually add the oil in a thin stream, until it is incorporated and the aioli is thick. Remove from food processor and add capers. Adjust the flavor with the pepper, to taste. Refrigerate aioli until you are ready to serve.

Chicken Stock

(Serves 2 quarts)

4 lbs. raw chicken carcasses
Salt
4 carrots
2 peeled onions
4 celery ribs
1 sprig parsley leaves
4 bay leaves

Place chicken pieces in a heavy stockpot and cover with cold water by at least 2 inches. Bring to a gentle simmer, over medium heat. Skim and remove the film that rises to the surface. As the chicken pieces simmer, add cold water to replace the water that has evaporated and continue skimming until broth is clear. Add the salt, vegetables and herbs. Return the liquid to a gentle simmer and continue to simmer for 2 hours. Pour broth in a colander over a large bowl. Discard the solids. Chill the liquid. When chilled, spoon off all traces of fat.

Citrus Balsamic Syrup

1 bottle (16 oz.) balsamic vinegar
6 oz. orange juice

In a saucepan, bring the balsamic vinegar and orange juice to a boil over medium heat. Boil until vinegar has reduced to about half. Mixture should be very syrupy, shiny and bubbling. Watch it very carefully; at this point it can burn easily. Remove from heat and let cool. This syrup will keep indefinitely in a tightly sealed jar at room temperature.

Serving suggestion: This syrup goes well with many foods, such as beef, chicken, pork chops, salmon, salads or roasted vegetables.

Crawfish Étouffée

(Serves 6)

1 lb. chopped crawfish tails
1 lb. Butter
2 T. flour
1 yellow onion, chopped
2 T. yellow pepper, chopped
1 garlic clove, minced
2 minced green onions
1 parsley bunch, minced
½ tsp. dry red chili flakes
½ tsp. salt

Melt butter and stir in flour. Add onion, pepper and garlic. Cook about 30 minutes. Add tails and cook 20 minutes. Add other ingredients and simmer about 20 to 30 minutes.

Serving suggestion: Étouffée is wonderful when served over rice.

Fish Broth

(Makes 1 quart)

1 chopped onion
¾ c. chopped leeks
2 sprigs parsley
4 chopped thyme sprigs
2 bay leaves
2 pounds fish trimmings
¾ cup white wine
6 cups cold water

In large saucepot, combine all ingredients except the water. Add just enough cold water to cover the ingredients by 2 inches. Bring to a simmer over moderate heat, skimming off any froth that floats to the top. Simmer the broth gently, about 30 minutes, until reduced to approx. 4 cups. Strain the broth through a fine sieve over a bowl and discard the solids.

Flavored Tomato Oil

1 c. olive oil
1 garlic clove, crushed
1 chopped shallot
¼ fennel bulb, chopped
1 T. chopped basil
3 T. tomato paste
Kosher salt

Heat 1 T. of olive oil in a medium-sized pan and add garlic, shallots, fennel and basil. Cover and sweat for 5 minutes over medium heat until the vegetables are tender. Add the tomato paste and mix well. Continue to cook for another 10 minutes. Gradually add the remaining oil, stirring continuously. Season well with kosher salt and cook gently for another 1½ hours. Let cool, then strain through a fine sieve. For an extra clear oil, strain twice through cheesecloth. Refrigerate to set the oil. Keep refrigerated.

Hollandaise Sauce

(Makes 1½ cups)

12 T. butter
3 egg yolks
1 T. lemon juice
1 T. chilled butter
1 T. heavy cream
Salt
White pepper

In a small, heavy pan over low heat, melt 12 tablespoons of butter without letting it brown. Set the butter aside and keep it warm. Off the heat, in a 2 quart stainless steel saucepan, beat the egg yolks with a wire whisk for 1 minute or until thick. Beat in the lemon juice. Then place the pan over very low heat and stir in 1 tablespoon of chilled butter with a whisk. Remove the pan from the heat and beat in the cream. Still off the heat, pour in the warm, melted butter by droplets, stirring constantly with the whisk. The sauce will thicken into a heavy cream. Taste the hollandaise; season with salt and white pepper.

Langoustine Broth

(Serves 8)

2 T. olive oil
2 lbs. langoustine shells
(you may substitute with shrimp or lobster shells)
2 oranges, quartered
1 tsp. saffron
2 whole pieces star anise
4 qt. cold water
1 can (28 oz.) peeled plum tomatoes in their juice
Fresh or dried bay leafs
4 garlic cloves
1 T. tomato paste

In a heavy roasting pan, heat the oil over moderate heat until hot. Add the shells and sear until they turn bright pink. Add the remaining ingredients and bring to a boil, uncovered. Continue to boil for 30 minutes. Ladle the broth into a colander, discarding the solids. Serve warm in small cups for appetizer or first course.

Pinot Noir Syrup

(Makes 2 cups)

½ c. sugar
2 c. Pinot Noir wine
1 sprig of rosemary

Place the sugar in a heavy bottomed saucepan, preferably nonstick and with rounded sides. Turn the heat to medium. Stir the sugar until it liquefies and begins to turn brown, about 10 minutes. Turn off the heat, stand back and carefully add the wine. Turn the heat to high and cook, stirring until the carmel mixture dissolves. Add the rosemary sprig and stir occasionally until the mixture is syrupy and reduced to just over 1/2 cup, 10 to 15 minutes. Let cool.

Serving suggestion: Spoon over fish, lamb, duck or a salad.

Preserved Lemon Saffron Reduction

4 c. chicken stock
2 T. butter
6 cloves garlic, crushed
2 finely chopped shallots
1 tsp. saffron
2 T. lemon juice
1 tsp. finely chopped lemon peel

Pour chicken stock into a saucepan, over medium heat. Reduce stock to half. In a sauté pan, melt butter, adding garlic, shallots, saffron, lemon juice and lemon peel. Sauté until garlic and shallots are golden brown. Transfer to chicken stock and simmer for 10 minutes.

Serving suggestions: This is a great, clean sauce for squab, Cornish hen or chicken.

Tropical Fruit Chutney

2 papaya - peeled, seeded and diced
2 mangoes - peeled, seeded and diced
3 Asian pears - cored and diced
1 lg. red onion - peeled and diced
2 Poblano peppers - seeded and diced
2 tsp. garlic, chopped
1 piece fresh ginger (approx. 3 in.), peeled and minced
3 oranges, zested and juiced
2 lemons, zested and juiced
2 oz. sugar
1 tsp. ground turmeric

In a heavy saucepan, sauté the red onion, garlic and ginger until onion is wilted. Add peppers and sauté about 1 minute. Add the sugar and turmeric, continuing to sauté until aromatic, about 1 minute. Add the fruit and juices and stir well to blend. Bring to boil then reduce heat to low and cook, stirring occasionally until fruit is barely cooked through and tender. If necessary, thicken lightly with cornstarch. Mixture should be thick.

Truffle Butter

(Makes 4 Tablespoons)

4 T. unsalted butter, softened
2 T. minced truffle peelings
½ tsp. kosher salt

On a small plate, mash the softened butter with a fork. Sprinkle with truffles and salt, distributing them as evenly as possible. Transfer the butter to a ramekin and cover. Refrigerate for up to 2 days. Serve at room temperature.

Truffle Mayonnaise

(Makes 1 cup)
1 c. olive oil
2 lg. Egg yolks
1 tsp. fresh lemon juice
1 tsp. Dijon mustard
¼ tsp. kosher salt
3 T. fresh truffles, finely minced

In a medium bowl, whisk egg yolks, lemon juice, mustard and salt until light and thick. Continuing to whisk, gradually add just a few drops of the oil. Do not add too much oil at the beginning or the mixture will not emulsify. As soon as the mixture begins to thicken, add the remaining oil in a slow, steady stream, whisking constantly. Stir in the minced truffles. Taste for seasoning and refrigerate.

Spice and Rubs

Spice and rubs are used to season meat, poultry and seafood. These mixtures are used to flavor food by making blends that result in fresher and tastier foods. You can rub the spice mixture onto the food or place the rub in a shallow bowl and dip the food directly into the rub. You can turn a rub into a paste by adding a little olive oil. The recipes in this section are sure to please your palate.

Health Tip: Discard any leftover rub that has come into contact with raw meat, poultry or fish.

Caribbean Rub

(Makes about ½ cup)

1 T. paprika
1 T. cayenne pepper
1 T. ground ginger
1 T. ground allspice
1 tsp. ground cinnamon
1 T. curry powder
1 T. sugar

Combine all the ingredients in a bowl. Store in a covered container.

Citrus Spice Mix

2 pieces star anise
2 cloves
½ tsp. pink peppercorns
1 tsp. allspice berries
2 T. ground dried orange peel

Combine the star anise, cloves, peppercorns and allspice berries in a small dry skillet and toast over medium heat until fragrant. Transfer to a spice grinder and grind fine. Add the ground orange peel and mix well.

Curry Powder

(Makes 5 Tablespoons)

2 whole, small dried red chili peppers
2 T. coriander seeds
1 T. cumin seeds
½ tsp. mustard seeds
1 tsp. peppercorns
½ tsp. ground turmeric

In a dry skillet, combine the chili peppers, coriander, cumin, mustard and peppercorn seeds. Place over medium heat and toast, shaking the pan often to prevent burning. Remove from the heat, transfer to a bowl and let cool to room temperature. Transfer the cooled spice mixture to a spice grinder or coffee mill. Grind to a fine powder. Transfer to a small bowl. Stir in the ground turmeric. Store in an airtight container in a cool place.

Dry Rose Petal Smoke Mix

16 oz. kosher salt
8 oz. brown sugar
1 T. ground coriander
1 T. ground allspice
1 T. dry rose petals

Combine ingredients.

Serving suggestion: Rub over fish fillets. Marinate about 6 hours before cooking.

This mix is suitable for smoking a variety of seafood and meats.

Dry Rub Spice

2 oz. fresh ground black pepper
½ tsp. cayenne
½ tsp. white pepper
1 tsp. ground cumin
1 tsp. dried oregano
2 oz. sweet paprika
1 tsp. ground allspice
½ tsp. celery seeds
1 - 2 T. chili powder

Combine ingredients and mix well. Sprinkle on item to be grilled or smoked and rub in lightly. Let stand for 30 minutes then cook as desired.

Four Spice Blend

(Makes 4 Teaspoons)
1 tsp. allspice
1 tsp. whole cloves
1 tsp. grated nutmeg
1 tsp. cinnamon

Individually, grind the allspice and cloves in a spice grinder or coffee mill. Combine the spices in a small bowl. Add the nutmeg and cinnamon. Store in a tightly sealed container.

Game Spice

1 T. juniper berries
1 T. allspice berries
1 tsp. pink peppercorns
1 T. coriander seed

Combine the juniper berries, allspice, pink peppercorns and coriander in a small dry skillet and toast over medium heat until fragrant. Transfer to a spice grinder and grind to a medium-fine powder.

Hot and Spicy Rub

(Makes 1/3 cup)

1 tsp. ground allspice
3 tsp. sugar
½ tsp. salt
¼ tsp. ground cinnamon
1 tsp. cayenne pepper
1 tsp. ground cumin
1 tsp. ground coriander
1 tsp. ground nutmeg

Combine all the ingredients in a bowl. Store in a covered container.

Indian Rub

(Makes about ½ cup)

1½ tsp. crushed red chili flakes
1 T. ground cumin seeds
2 T. ground coriander
1 tsp. ground fennel seeds
1 tsp. ground mustard seeds
1 T. ground turmeric
1 tsp. curry powder

Combine all the ingredients in a bowl. Store in a covered container.

Pickling Spice

(Makes ½ cup)

5 bay leaves
1 cinnamon stick
2 star anise
2 T. allspice berries
2 tsp. cloves
2 T. pink peppercorns
1 T. coriander seeds
2 tsp. cardamon seeds

Break the bay leaves, cinnamon stick and star anise into pieces. Roughly chop all the other ingredients. Combine and store in a sealed jar.

Entrée

These flavorful recipes offer a full range of simple, yet fabulous, main entrées. When preparing these wonderful dishes, you'll discover the unique chemistry between the ingredients. The recipes are all very impressive and easy to prepare. Here you will learn how to slow-cook, roast, sauté and grill extraordinarily seafood, birds and meats.

Braised Lamb Shanks with White Beans

(Serves 4)

4 lamb shanks (about 12 oz. each)
1 T. olive oil
2 c. chopped onions
1 can (28 oz.) whole tomatoes in juice
1 tsp. dried rosemary leaves, crumbled
4 cloves garlic, peeled and crushed
1 T. all-purpose flour
1 c. beef broth
1 can (15 oz.) cannellini beans, rinsed and drained

Heat oil in a 5-quart, non-aluminum pot or Dutch oven over medium-high heat. Add shanks in batches and brown on all sides, about 10 minutes. Remove to a plate. Add onion to pot and cook for 5 minutes, stirring often, until softened. Return shanks to pot. Add tomatoes, rosemary and garlic. In a small bowl, mix flour with 1 cup broth until well blended. Stir into pot. Cover and simmer for 1½ hours or until meat is tender. Add beans to pot. Cover and simmer 15 minutes or until beans are hot.

Carrot Risotto

(Serves 4)

1 medium onion, chopped
1 T. olive oil
1 tsp. minced garlic
1 c. risotto
2 c. chicken stock
1¾ c. water
1 c. carrot juice
1/3 c. freshly grated Parmesan
Salt to taste

Cook onion and oil in a 2-quart saucepan over medium heat, stirring until onions are soft. Add garlic and cook, stirring, for 30 seconds. Add risotto, chicken stock and water. Bring to a boil. Reduce heat, simmer and cover, until risotto is tender, for about 20 minutes. Add carrot juice and simmer until creamy. Stir in Parmesan and salt to taste.

Chicken with Scallion Ginger Sauce

(Serves 4)

4 chicken breast halves, boneless and skinless
1 T. minced ginger
½ c. olive oil
¼ c. scallions, trimmed and chopped
Salt
2 T. soy sauce
1 tsp. sesame oil

Steam the chicken over simmering water for 10 to 15 minutes. The chicken is done when it is white and firm to the touch. Meanwhile, stir together the ginger, oil, and scallions in a bowl. Salt to taste. The mixture should be quite strong. When the chicken is done, drizzle it with the soy sauce and sesame oil and serve. Divide the scallion-ginger sauce into four small bowls for dipping.

Cremini Mushroom, Apple, Potato Cake

(Serves 6)

3 T. olive oil
1 lb. chopped cremini mushroom caps
1 finely chopped white onion
1 tart apple
1 tsp. chopped fresh thyme
1 tsp. chopped fresh tarragon
1 tsp. salt
½ tsp. ground cumin seed
1 lb. Potatoes
Preheat over to 450º.

Heat 1-tablespoon oil in a 10 inch sauté pan, over moderately high heat. Add mushrooms and onion. Sauté, stirring until browned. Transfer to a bowl. Peel and grate apple and stir into mushrooms with thyme, tarragon, salt and cumin. Peel potatoes and grate. Toss with mushroom mixture. Heat 2-tablespoons oil in sauté pan over moderately high heat. Add mushroom-potato mixture, spreading in an even layer in sauté pan. Sauté for 1 minute. Put sauté pan in middle of oven and bake for 20 minutes. Carefully slide cake onto a platter. The cake should be golden brown on top and tender when pierced with a fork.

Kalan Soibelman

Curry, Saffron Oil-Roasted Cornish Hens

(Serves 6)

3 Cornish hens
¼ c. olive oil
1½ T. curry powder
½ tsp. saffron
2½ tsp. salt

Preheat oven to 475º.

Heat a roasting pan over medium heat with ½-tablespoon olive oil. In a bowl, stir together olive oil, curry powder, saffron and salt. Rinse hens and pat dry. Tie drumsticks together. Brush the spice oil over the hens. Transfer hens to the roasting pan and sear on both sides. Place in oven and cook until tender, about 30 to 40 minutes. Transfer hens to a cutting board and halve each lengthwise along backbone.

Serving suggestions: Serve with sautéed greens and risotto.

Filet of Beef with Plum Puree Sauce

(Serves 4)

4 - 6 oz. beef filet medallions
Salt and pepper

Filet medallions can be broiled or pan-grilled if you prefer. When grill is ready, grill medallions 2 minutes per side for rare, or 1 to 2 minutes longer for medium-rare to medium. Season the steak, as it cooks, with salt and pepper. Serve steaks with plum puree sauce.

Plum Puree Sauce

4 plumes, medium sized
1 T. fresh lemon juice
2 T. minced fresh parsley

Plunge the plums into boiling water for about 30 seconds, or until the skin loosens. Then plunge them into cold ice water, to stop the cooking process. Remove skin with a paring knife. Cut fruit into halves and remove pits. Puree the plums in a blender and add lemon juice and parsley until mixture forms a sauce.

Garlic Crusted Rack of Lamb

2 T. olive oil
1 rack of lamb (12 cutlets)
6 cloves garlic, chopped
1 bunch Italian flat-leaf parsley, chopped
4 c. Panko bread crumbs
Salt and pepper

Remove the excess fat from the lamb. Heat a frying pan over high heat, add the lamb and cook for 3 minutes or until meat is sealed. Remove from the pan and set aside. To make the garlic crust: combine the garlic, parsley, bread crumbs and oil - spread mixture over the lamb. Place in a baking dish. Bake lamb for 12-15 minutes or until lamb is cooked to your liking.

Serving suggestion: Place hot ***lemon and arugala risotto*** on a serving plate, top with a lamb chop.

Lemon and Arugala Risotto

5½ c. ***vegetable stock***
2 T. oil
2 c. Arborio rice
2 T. grated lemon rind
6½ oz. baby arugala leaves (no stems)
Cracked black pepper
Kosher salt
Parmesan shavings

Place the vegetable stock in a saucepan over medium-high heat and bring to a boil, then reduce to a simmer. Heat the oil in another saucepan over medium-high heat. Add the rice to the oil and cook for 1 minute. Add the stock, 2 cups at a time, stirring frequently and continue adding cups of stock and stirring until all the stock has been absorbed and the rice is tender. Season with salt and pepper. Fold in the lemon rind and arugala leaves. Top with Parmesan shavings.

Morel Mushroom Custard

3 egg yolks
2 eggs
¼ c. sugar
1 c. milk
1 c. heavy cream
1 tsp. morel mushroom powder
1/3 c. goat cheese
Salt
Preheat oven to 350°.

Whisk the egg yolks, eggs and sugar in a bowl until pale and creamy. Heat the milk, cream and morel mushroom powder over medium heat and slowly pour into egg mixture. While mixture is still warm, add the soft goat cheese and mix well. Pour custard into 4 ramekins and dust with salt. Place the ramekins in a baking dish, half-filled with water. Place in the oven and cook for 30-40 minutes. Remove from the oven and let cool.

Serving suggestion: The custard is wonderful when served with ***seared foie gras***.

Oven-Braised Beef Short Ribs

(Serves 4)

3 lbs. beef short ribs
1¼ cups all-purpose flour, seasoned with salt and pepper, for dredging
¼ c. olive oil
1 lg. onion, chopped
1 lg. green pepper, chopped
2 med. carrots, chopped
4 lg. garlic cloves, minced
1 c. dry red wine
1½ T. tomato paste
1 can (14.5 oz.) whole tomatoes broken apart, with juices
¾ c. beef stock
1 bay leaf
1 tsp. dried thyme
2 T. fresh parsley, chopped (or 1 T. dried)
Salt and pepper to taste
Preheat oven to 350°.

Lightly coat the ribs with the flour, shaking off excess. Heat the oil in an ovenproof sauté pan, large enough to hold the ribs in one layer, over high heat. Add the ribs and brown on all sides, about 3 minutes per side. Remove the ribs and reduce heat to medium-high. Add the onion, green pepper and carrots to the pan; sauté until lightly browned, about 5 minutes. Add the garlic and sauté one additional minute. Pour in the wine and cook briefly, scraping any browned bits from bottom of pan. Add the tomato paste and stir well to combine. Add the remaining ingredients, and then return the browned ribs to the pan, making certain they are on the bottom, in a single layer. Baste the ribs with the sauce. Cover pan with a tight lid or foil. Place in oven and cook for about 2 hours or until the ribs fall apart easily with a fork. Check about every 30 minutes and baste. Remove pan from oven. Skim any visible fat from the pan. (If necessary, remove ribs from pan to skim the fat). Discard the bay leaf. If desired, further reduce the sauce over high heat.

Serving suggestion: Scoop the sauce and vegetables over each rib and accompany with a side dish of risotto, rice or pasta.

Rabbit Stuffed with Plums

(Serves 4)

12 plums, pitted
2 c. port wine
3 lb. cleaned rabbit
1 tsp. kosher salt
1 tsp. black pepper
1 T. chopped thyme
1 T. chopped sage
½ tsp. olive oil

At least 6 hours before cooking, combine the plums and port wine in a medium bowl and let stand until plums are soft and have absorbed most of the wine. Drain the wine from the plums and reserve.

Preheat the oven to 450°.

Lay the rabbit on it's back. Sprinkle the cavity with salt, pepper, thyme and sage. Stuff the cavity with the plums. Drizzle the reserved wine over the plums. With needle and thread, sew together the flaps to enclose the stuffing. Place the rabbit on rack, set in a shallow roasting pan. Roast the rabbit for 30 minutes. Reduce the heat to 350°. Baste frequently with the wine and natural juices. If rabbit starts to dry, add some water to the pan. Cook rabbit for an additional 20 to 25 minutes. Place rabbit on a cutting board and let rest for about 10 minutes. Scoop out the stuffing and place on a plate. Carve rabbit and arrange around the plums. Pour juices over rabbit and serve.

Roasted Squab

2 tsp. garlic powder
2 tsp. cumin, ground
2 tsp. turmeric
½ c. olive oil
2 Squabs (approx. 3 oz. each)
Preheat the oven to 400°.

In a bowl, mix the garlic powder, cumin, turmeric and olive oil. Brush the squabs, inside and out, with the spiced olive oil. With a sauté pan over medium heat, add the squabs and cook for 2-3 minutes. Turn the squabs when seared on all sides. Transfer to preheated oven and roast for 8 minutes. Remove squab and serve hot.

Seafood Paella

6 small rock-lobster tails
12 large raw shrimp
6 cherry stone clams
6 mussels
½ lb. chorizo or other garlic-flavored sausage
2/3 c. olive oil
½ lb. pork cubes
4 chicken breasts, thighs and legs
1 onion
1 green pepper
¼ c. tomato sauce
3 c. long grain rice
1/8 tsp. saffron powder
1 tsp. salt
1 tsp. garlic powder
¼ tsp. pepper
1½ qt. boiling water
1 c. peas
1 fresh tomato, peeled, seeded and diced

With kitchen shears, clip centers of ribs on belly side of lobster shells. Loosen meat from shells with fingers; leave meat attached near tail fins. Shell and devein shrimp. Scrub clams and mussels. Soak mussels in cold water for 30 minutes to remove salty taste. Discard any that open their shells while soaking. Drain. Place sausage and pork cubes in shallow skillet, cover with water and bring to a boil. Boil 5 minutes; drain. Remove skin; cut into ¼ inch rounds. Heat 1/3 cups oil. Fry sausage until browned on all sides and no longer pink. Remove from skillet; drain. Add chicken to skillet. Fry 45 minutes or until golden brown and meat is cooked. Remove from skillet; drain. Add lobster to skillet; fry just until shells start to turn pink. Remove from skillet; drain. Add remaining oil to skillet; heat thoroughly. Peel and chop onion; sauté in skillet 10 minutes or until tender. Remove seeds and membranes from green pepper; dice. Add to onions; sauté 5 minutes. Stir in tomato sauce; simmer until mixture thickens and holds its shape in a spoon. Add rice, saffron, salt, garlic powder and pepper; mix well. Add boiling water; mix well. Bring mixture to boil; reduce heat to simmer. Arrange lobster, shrimp, clams, mussels, sausage, pork, and chicken on top of rice mixture. Scatter peas and tomatoes over rice and meat; cover. Simmer 30-45 minutes or until rice is tender, shrimp and lobster meat turn white and mussels and clams pop open. Remove from heat. Cover; let rest 10 minutes for flavors to mingle. Serve from the pan.

Slow-Cooked Spare Ribs

(Serves 4)

2 lbs. pork spare ribs, cut into pieces
¼ c. soy sauce
1 star anise
1 dried chili
6 slices fresh ginger
4 crushed garlic cloves
2 tsp. sugar

Combine the pork ribs, soy sauce, star anise, chili, ginger, garlic, cloves and sugar with 1/2 cup water in a skillet just enough to hold the meat. Bring to a boil, then turn the heat to low, cover and simmer for 2 hours, turning the meat occasionally and adding water a little at a time, if and when the pan dries out. The meat is done when it is tender and nearly falling from the bone. Remove the meat, spoon some or all of the juices over it and serve.

Spiced Braised Leg of Lamb

(Serves 6)

1 leg of lamb, bone in (about 7 pounds)
4 T. olive oil
1½ c. ***beef stock***
Salt and pepper
1 tsp. ground coriander seeds
3 tsp. ground cumin seeds
2 tsp. curry powder
Preheat oven to 250º.

In a small bowl, combine the spices. Rub the mixture over the surface of the lamb. In a cast iron casserole, heat the oil over moderate heat until hot but not smoking. Add the lamb and brown lightly on all sides. Do not let the spices burn. Pour the stock around the lamb. Add salt and pepper. Cover with foil, this will keep the meat from drying out. Place casserole in the center of the oven. Braise, basting every 30 minutes, until the meat is very tender. Remove lamb from the oven and carve it into pieces. Keep warm on a serving plate. Strain the sauce through a fine sieve into a saucepan. Place the pan in the refrigerator for 30 minutes to allow the fat to rise to the top. Remove and discard the fat. Warm the sauce and transfer to a sauceboat. Serve the lamb, passing the sauce.

Steamed Black Mussels

(Serves 2)

2 lbs. black mussels
2 oz. shaved fennel
1 oz. garlic cloves, thinly sliced
2 oz. sliced chorizo
½ oz. olive oil
1 qt. clam juice
1 T. saffron
2 oz. diced tomato

Combine fennel, garlic and chorizo in a sauté pan. Sauté with oil, over medium high heat until golden brow, about 2 min. To prepare saffron broth, heat clam juice in a sauce pan. Bring to a boil; add saffron and salt to taste. Add mussels, tomato and saffron broth to sauté pan. When mussels fully open, arrange in bowl.

Striped Bass Braised with Leeks

(Serves 4)

1½ lbs. leeks, washed, trimmed and chopped
½ c. white wine
Salt to taste
Pepper to taste
1 T. Dijon mustard
1½ lbs. striped bass
Preheat the oven to 400°.

Scatter the leeks over the bottom of an ovenproof casserole dish. Mix in the wine, salt and mustard. Top with the fish. Sprinkle the fish with salt and pepper. Cover the casserole dish. Bake for 10 to 15 minutes, or until a thin-bladed knife meets little or no resistance when inserted into the fish. Uncover and serve the fish with the leeks and pan juices spooned over it.

Sweet Corn Flan

(Serves 4)

3 ears shucked, fresh corn
2/3 c. 1% milk
2 lg. eggs
Dash of salt
½ tsp. cayenne
2 T. chopped chives
Preheat oven to 350°.

Cook corn in a pot of boiling water until tender, about 5 minutes. Drain and cool. Cut off kernels with a sharp knife into a bowl, scraping ears. Reserve 3/4 cup of corn for relish and puree remainder in a blender with the milk until smooth. Force corn puree through a fine sieve into a bowl, discarding skins. Whisk together eggs, salt, cayenne and chives until blended. Whisk in corn puree. Pour flan mixture into lightly oiled ramekins and bake in a hot-water bath, just until set, about 40 minutes. Remove ramekins from water bath and cool on a rack. Chill until cold, about 2 hours.

Tequila Duck Confit

8 dried juniper berries
1 tsp. pink peppercorns
2 T. kosher salt
2 tsp. chopped tarragon leaves
1 crumbled bay leaf
3 allspice berries
½ tsp. sugar
1 tsp. tequila
4 Moulard duck legs

To make the seasoning, in a spice grinder, combine the first 7 ingredients. Rub the spice mixture and tequila into the duck legs and place in a plastic dish. Cover with plastic wrap and refrigerate overnight.

Preheat the oven to 300º.

Arrange duck legs on heavy-duty foil. Fold the foil over the legs and crease the corners. Make sure it is a tightly sealed. Place the package on a baking sheet pan and bake for 2 hours. Remove from the oven and allow to rest. Carefully unfold the package with tongs and serve.

Veal Steak

(Serves 4)

4 T. butter
4 pieces veal flank steak, trimmed
Kosher salt to taste
Ground black pepper to taste
1 tsp. thyme
1 tsp. saffron
4 T. heavy whipping cream

Divide the butter between two skillets that are large enough to hold two steaks each and place over moderate heat until hot. Very lightly season the veal with salt and pepper. Sear the veal gently until it is cooked through but still tender, 5 to 6 minutes on each side. Remove the veal to a warm platter. Add 2 tablespoons of cream and saffron to each pan to deglaze it and pour the sauce over the steaks. Season with thyme and let the meat rest before carving across the grain and serving.

Venison Medallions

(Serves 4)

1 lb. venison loin, cut into medallions
2 T. walnut oil
Sweet citrus salt

Add the oil to a large skillet and turn the heat to medium-high. One or two minutes later, add the venison and turn the heat up, to high. Season the meat with the sweet citrus salt and cook until nicely browned, about 2 minutes. Turn the meat and lower the heat to medium. Continue to cook, turning once or twice, until medium-rare, about 6 minutes.

Desserts

Dessert is the titillating part of any meal. Presentation is everything and some of these recipes are sure to raise a few eyebrows. Satisfying and soothing, meant to tease the receptors on your palate. Learn the secrets to these gourmet treats.

Almond Biscotti

2 c. flour
¾ c. sugar
2 tsp. baking powder
½ tsp. cinnamon
¼ tsp. salt
1½ c. slivered almonds
3 large eggs
2 tsp. vanilla extract
Preheat oven to 350º.

In a bowl, mix flour, sugar, baking powder, cinnamon and salt. Stir in the almonds. In a separate bowl, whisk the eggs and vanilla. Stir the egg mixture into the flour mixture. Knead the dough, folding until smooth. The dough may look dry, but it will come together as it is kneaded. Divide dough in half and shape into 12-inch long logs. Press log down until flatten, about 2 inches wide and 1 inch high. Transfer to a parchment lined baking sheet. Bake the logs for 30 minutes, or until risen and firm. Place baking sheet onto a cooling rack. When the logs have cooled completely, cut the logs diagonally into 1/4 inch thick slices. Place slices on a parchment paper covered baking sheet and place in oven at 350º and bake for an additional 10 to 15 minutes, or until biscotti are crisp and golden brown. Let cool and serve.

Anise Tuiles

3 egg whites
¾ c. sugar
1/3 c. flour
½ c. butter, melted
¾ tsp. anise extract
Preheat the oven to 350°.

Line a baking sheet with wax paper. Combine melted butter and sugar; whip until creamy. Fold in the flour and add anise extract. Place spoonfuls of batter on the lined baking sheet, and then spread it out as thinly as possible with a spatula. Bake for 10 minutes, and then remove with the spatula while still hot. Cut out circles, using a 4-inch circular pastry cutter. Shape by molding each circle to the inside of a champagne flute. Leave in position to cool.

Serving suggestion: Fill with sorbet or gelato.

Carmel Mousse

1 tsp. unflavored gelatin
8 T. cold water
2 T. dark rum
¾ c. brown sugar
6 lg. egg yolks
2 c. heavy cream

Dissolve gelatin in 4 T. of cold water, stir and set aside. Melt sugar in a saucepan over low heat, stirring with a spoon. As soon as the sugar has melted, remove from the heat. Stir in the remaining 2 T. cold water. The water will cause the sugar to bubble and sizzle. Keep stirring to dissolve the lumps. Add gelatin mixture and keep stirring. In a bowl, beat the egg yolks with an electric mixer until they thicken. Pour in the sugar-gelatin mixture and beat until the mousse is cool. This step should take about 5 to 10 minutes. Whip the heavy cream in a large bowl until it peaks. Fold the whipped cream into the mousse. Chill the mousse for at least 1 hour before serving.

Cognac Lemon Curd

(Makes 1 cup)

½ c. fresh lemon juice
1 tsp. cognac
12 T. sugar
2 egg yolks
1 egg white, whipped
Lemon zest

In a bowl, combine lemon juice, cognac, sugar, egg yolks and lemon zest. Set the bowl in a water bath, over medium heat. Cook curd, whisking occasionally for about 5 minutes. Strain into a bowl and allow to cool. Fold in whipped egg whites. Refrigerate until ready to use.

Dried Plum Tea Bread

1½ c. California dried plums, chopped
Grated zest and juice of 1 lemon
2/3 c. butter
¾ c. sugar
2 eggs
2 T. milk
1½ c. flour
½ c. chopped walnuts
Preheat oven to 350°.

In a large bowl, cream the butter and sugar until fluffy. Gradually beat in the eggs, milk, lemon zest and lemon juice. Mix the flour and chopped walnuts into the cream mixture. Fold in the chopped plums. Pour mixture into a non-stick bread pan and smooth the top with a spatula. Bake for 55 - 60 minutes, or until a wooden toothpick inserted in the center of the tea bread comes out clean. Transfer the tea bread to a cooling rack and allow to cool in the pan for 10 minutes. Invert the tea bread onto a rack, remove the pan and cool to room temperature. The tea bread is best served in very thin slices.

Espresso Granite

1¼ c. cold brewed espresso
¼ c. skim milk
¼ c. simple syrup (or substitute Karo syrup)

Pour all of the ingredients into a metal pan and stir to combine. Place the pan, uncovered, in the freezer and freeze until solid. When you are ready to serve, use the edge of a spoon to scrape the granite. The texture should look like shaved ice.

Serving suggestion: Serve with chocolate tart, cake or by itself.

Fig Compote

2 c. water
1 c. sugar
½ c. white wine
1 tsp. cinnamon
1 T. of orange juice
½ tsp. vanilla extract
6 oz. of figs

Combine all of the ingredients, except the figs, in a saucepan over medium heat and simmer. Add the figs. Simmer until figs are tender. Spoon figs onto a plate and top with the syrup.

Serving suggestion: Serve with gelato or pie.

Marzipan Creations

1 lb. almond paste
1 lb. sifted sugar
1/3 c. corn syrup

In a food processor, add almond paste and sugar. Pulse until the mixture is very fine. Add the corn syrup and pulse a few times to bring mixture together. Do not over mix. Remove marzipan and knead by hand. Wrap marzipan with plastic wrap and place in an airtight container. Store in a dry place until needed.

With the marzipan you can create fruits, vines and leaves to decorate cakes or your favorite desserts. For painting your pieces, use food based paints that are brushed on dry.

Mint Sugar

2 oz. mint leaves, without stems (approx. 2 bunches)
2 c. sugar
1/3 c. cold water

Blend mint leaves in food processor for 2 minutes. Add sugar and water. Blend until smooth. Keep refrigerated.

Serving suggestion: Use as a dessert topping.

Plum Truffle Tempura

8 oz. bittersweet chocolate, chopped
1 c. California dried plum, chopped fine
½ c. heavy cream
1 T. dark rum
1 T. cognac

Bring cream to a simmer in a medium saucepan. Remove from the heat and stir in rum and cognac. Whisk in chocolate until it melts and ganache is smooth. Stir in dried plums. Pour ganache into a plastic wrap lined pie pan and chill, uncovered until firm. About 2-3 hours. Scoop ganache with a small melon baller to form small balls.

Tempura Mixture

4 eggs
2 c. flour
1 T. cinnamon
2 T. sugar
4 c. olive oil

Beat the eggs in a small bowl. In a separate bowl, combine flour, cinnamon and sugar.

Drop a ganache ball into the flour mixture, then the egg mixture. Repeat this process so that each ganache ball is dipped twice. Place oil in a saucepot over medium heat. Drop ball into oil until lightly golden brown, for about 1/2 a minute. Remove ball and serve hot.

Rum Cocoa Mousse

3/4 c. sugar
4 T. dark rum
6 lg. egg yolks
1 T. cocoa powder
2 c. heavy cream

Place sugar in a heavy saucepan over high heat and cook, stirring with a wooden spoon. Cook until the sugar turns a deep, dark carmel color. As soon as the carmel is the right color, add the rum. Be cautious and stand back, the rum will cause the carmel to bubble and sizzle. Keep stirring to dissolve the lumps. When there are no longer any bubbles, set aside. Beat the egg yolks with an electric mixer on high speed until the yolks thicken and turn a pale yellow. Reduce the speed and pour in the carmel mixture, add the cocoa powder. Beat for 5 minutes to cool the mousse. In a large bowl, whip the heavy cream until it holds soft peaks. Using a rubber spatula, fold the whipped cream into the mousse. Chill the mousse for 1 hour before serving.

Vanilla Mango Custard

3 egg yolks
2 eggs
¼ c. sugar
1 c. milk
1 c. heavy cream
1 tsp. vanilla extract
1/3 c. cream cheese
1½ c. chopped mango
Preheat oven to 350°.

In a bowl, whisk the egg yolks, eggs and sugar, until pale and creamy. Heat the milk, cream and vanilla over medium heat. Slowly pour into egg mixture. While mixture is still warm, add the cream cheese and mix well. Place the mango in the bottom of 4 ramekins in a baking dish that is half-filled with water. Place in the oven and cook for 30-40 minutes. Remove from the oven and let cool.

Serving suggestion: Place fresh fruit on top of the custard and add whipped cream.

Warm Plum Chocolate Baby Cake

1½ c. butter
6 oz. bittersweet chocolate
1 T. unsweetened cocoa powder
1 T. instant espresso powder
6 eggs
1 c. dark brown sugar
1 c. flour
1 tsp. vanilla extract
1 tsp. lemon zest
½ c. chopped California dried plums
Preheat oven to 350º.

In a plastic mixing bowl, melt the butter and chocolate in the microwave oven. With an electric mixer, beat the cocoa powder, espresso powder and eggs until fluffy. Add sugar, flour, vanilla extract and lemon zest. Beat for 1 minute and fold in chopped dried plums. Add melted butter and chocolate to mixture. Beat for 1 minute. Transfer the mixture to small buttered muffin forms. Bake for 5 to 8 minutes. The baby cakes should be firm on the outside, but still soft and creamy on the inside. Serve the baby cake warm.

Serving suggestion: This plum chocolate baby cake is wonderful with lightly whipped cream and candied lemon peel. It is also great with vanilla bean ice cream.

White Chocolate Vanilla Bean Foam

2 vanilla beans, halved lengthwise
¼ c. sugar
1 can (13 oz.) coconut milk
½ lb. bittersweet white chocolate
½ c. heavy cream

Scrape seeds from the vanilla beans, with the point of a paring knife, into a 2-quart saucepan with the sugar. Cook over moderately low heat. Stir constantly until sugar is melted. Add coconut milk and chocolate. Simmer, stirring occasionally, until sugar and chocolate have dissolved. Pour into a metal bowl and stir in cream. Set metal bowl in a large bowl of ice and cold water to chill, stirring occasionally. Transfer sauce to a CO2 canister and tightly seal. Unscrew charge holder from head and put in a charger. Reattach charge holder and screw on tightly. Chill filled canister at least 1 hour to produce a stiff foam.

Serving suggestion: This sweet chocolate foam is wonderful on top of desserts or can be served with fresh berries.

Common Measurements and Equivalents

½ teaspoon	=	30 drops
1 teaspoon	=	1/3 tablespoon or 60 drops
3 teaspoon	=	1 tablespoon
½ tablespoon	=	1 ½ teaspoons
1 tablespoon	=	3 teaspoons or ½ fluid ounce
2 tablespoon	=	1/8 cup or 1 fluid ounce
3 tablespoon	=	1 ½ fluid ounces or 1 jigger
4 tablespoon	=	¼ cup or 2 fluid ounces
5 1/3 tablespoons	=	1/3 cup or 5 tablespoons + 1 teaspoon
8 tablespoons	=	½ cup or 4 fluid ounces
10 2/3 tablespoons	=	2/3 cup or 10 tablespoons + 2 teaspoons
12 tablespoons	=	¾ cup or 6 fluid ounces
16 tablespoons	=	1 cup or 8 fluid ounces or ½ pint
1/8 cup	=	2 tablespoons or 1 fluid ounce
¼ cup	=	4 tablespoons or 2 fluid ounces
1/3 cup	=	5 tablespoons + 1 teaspoon
3/8 cup	=	¼ cup + 2 tablespoons
½ cup	=	8 tablespoons or 4 fluid ounces
2/3 cup	=	10 tablespoons plus 2 teaspoons
5/8 cup	=	½ cup + 2 tablespoons
¾ cup	=	12 tablespoons or ½ pint or 8 fluid ounces
7/8 cup	=	¾ cup + 2 tablespoons
1 cup	=	16 tablespoons or ½ pint or 8 fluid ounces
2 cups	=	1 pint or 16 fluid ounces
1 pint	=	2 cups or 16 fluid ounces
1 quart	=	2 pints or 4 cups or 32 fluid ounces
1 gallon	=	4 quarts or 8 pints or 16 cups or 128 fluid ounces

Oven Temperature Terminology

Very slow	250 – 300°
Slow	300 – 325°
Moderate	350 – 375°
Very hot	450 – 475°
Extremely hot	500 – 525°

Measurement Conversions

c.	cup	*pkg.*	package
tsp.	teaspoon	*pkgs.*	packages
T.	tablespoon	*pt.*	pint(s)
lb.	pound	*qt.*	quart(s)
lbs.	pounds	*gal.*	gallon
oz.	ounce	*env.*	envelope(s)
sm.	small	*ctn.*	container/carton(s)
med.	medium	*opt.*	optional
lg.	large	*doz.*	dozen

Food Definitions

Aioli (Ay-oh-lee) A strongly flavored garlic mayonnaise.

Arugula (Ah-Roo-guh-lah) An aromatic salad green with a peppery mustard flavor.

Biscotti (Bee-skawt-tee) A twice-baked Italian biscuit (cookie).

Carpaccio (Kahr-PAH-chee-oh) Carpaccio consists of thin shavings of raw beef or fish.

Cavier (KA-vee-ahr) This is an elegant and expensive salted fish roe (eggs). Sturgeon roe is premium and considered the "true" cavier.

Cepes (Sehp) Large, strongly flavored mushrooms, ranging in color from yellow-brown to reddish brown.

Compote (Kahm-poht) A chilled dish of fresh or dried fruit that has been slowly cooked in a sugar syrup.

Confit (Kohn-Fee) This specialty of France, is a method of preserving meat, whereby it is salted and slowly cooked in it's own fat.

Crème Fraiche (Krehm Fresh) In France crème fraiche is a specialty; the cream is unpasteurized and can range from that of commercial sour cream.

Crouton (Kroo-tawn) A small piece or cube of bread that has been browned, either by sautéing or baking.

Emulsion (Ih-MUHL-shuhn) Emulsifying is done by slowly (drop-by drop) adding one ingredient to another while at the same time mixing rapidly.

Etouffee (Ay-too-fay) This popular Cajun dish is a thick, spicy stew of crayfish and vegetables served over white rice.

Flan (Flahn) A custard or fruit or savory filling.

Foie Gras (FWAH GRAH) Foie gras is the term generally used for goose liver.

Frittata (Frih-Tah-tuh) An Italian omelet.

Ganache (Gahn-Ahsh) A rich chocolate consisting of semisweet chocolate and whipping cream.

Gazpacho (Gahz-PAH-choh) A refreshingly cold, summertime soup.

Gelato (Jeh-LAH-toh) The Italian word for "ice cream".

Granite (Grah-nee-tay) A frozen mixture of water, sugar and liquid flavoring such as fruit juice, wine or coffee.

Gravlax (Grahv-lahks) A Swedish specialty of raw salmon cured in salt and sugar.

Kaffir lime Grown in Southwest Asia or Hawaii, the tree produces small, pear-shaped citrus fruit and the skin is bright yellow-green, bumpy and wrinkled.

Langoustine (Lahn-goo-steen) The French word for prawn.

Mesclun (MEHS-kluhn) Mesclun (also called salad mix and gourmet salad mix) is simply a potpourri of young, small salad greens.

Marzipan (Mahr-zih-pan) A sweet, pliable mixture of almond paste, sugar and sometimes-unbeaten egg whites.

Morel (Muh-Rehl) Belongs to the same fungus species as the truffle, wild mushrooms.

Mousse (Moos) A French term meaning froth or foam.

Paella (Pi-Ay-yuh) A Spanish dish of saffron flavored rice combined with meats, shellfish and vegetables.

Phyllo (Fee-loh) This refers to tissue-thin layers of pastry dough.

Quail (Kwayl) The American quail is white and delicately flavored. Quail is a young game bird.

Risotto (Rih-Saw-toh) An Italian rice specialty.

Saffron (Saf-ruhn) Saffron is the most expensive spice. This comes from the yellow-orange stigma of a small purple crocus flower. Each flower provides only three stigmas.

Sieve (Sihn) To strain liquid or particles of food through the mesh or perforated holes of a sieve or strainer.

Squab (Skwahb) A young, 4 week old domesticated pigeon.

Tartar (Tar-Tar) A dish of coarsely ground or finely chopped high-quality, raw fish or lean beef.

Truffle (TRUHF-uhl; Troo-fuhl) One of the rarest and most expensive (mushrooms) foods in the world. Truffles, coming from France, are often called "black diamonds", and are found growing wild under oak trees.

Tuile (Tweel) A thin, crisp cookie.

Venison (Vehn-ih-suhn) Large game meat, commonly thought of as deer.

Helpful Cooking Hints

Seeds and nuts, both shelled and unshelled, keep best and longest when stored in the freezer. Unshelled nuts crack more easily when frozen. Nuts and seeds can be used directly from the freezer.

Cheeses should be served at room temperature, approximately 70º.

Fresh lemon juice will remove onion scent from hands.

A lump of sugar added to water when cooking greens helps vegetables retain their fresh color.

To cut down on odors when cooking cabbage, cauliflower, etc., add a little vinegar to the cooking water.

To avoid tears when cutting onions, try briefly placing them in the freezer before cutting.

To keep hot oil from splattering, sprinkle a little salt or flour in the pan before frying.

A few drops of lemon juice added to simmering rice will keep the grains separated.

A little vinegar or lemon juice added to potatoes before draining will make them extra white when mashed.

Tomatoes added to meats will help to naturally tenderize them. Tomatoes contain an acid that works well to break down meats.

Whenever possible, cut meats across the grain, they will have a nice appearance and be easier to eat.

Thaw all meat, seafood and poultry in the refrigerator for maximum safety. Never leave meat, seafood or poultry at room temperature for more than two hours.

Lemon juice, rubbed on fish before cooking, will enhance the flavor and help maintain a good color.

To make self-rising flour, mix 4 cups flour, 2 teaspoons salt and 2 tablespoons baking powder and store in a tightly cover container.

When in doubt, always sift flour before measuring.

To make bread crumbs, toast the heels of bread and chop in a blender or food processor.

Dust a baking pan or work surface with flour by filling an empty salt shaker with flour.

Egg whites need to be at room temperature for greater volume when whipped.

When grating citrus peels, bits of peel are often stuck in the holes of the grater. You can easily brush it off by using a clean toothbrush.

Cut-up dried fruit sometimes sticks to the blade of your knife. To prevent this problem, coat the blade of your knife with a thing film of vegetable spray before cutting.

To make a simple polish for copper bottom cookware, mix equal parts of flour and salt with vinegar to create a paste. Store the paste in the refrigerator.

Food storage: Refrigerator, 36 - 40°. Freezer, 0° or lower.

About the Author

As a young boy, I loved to experiment in the kitchen. When I started my career, I cooked in small restaurants and worked my way up into professional kitchens. Along the way, I attended courses at the California Culinary Academy and the Culinary Institute of America.

My cooking style has been deeply influenced by world flavors. French, Italian, Mediterranean, Asian and American to name just a few.

Good food is clearly an emotional and spiritual encounter, one that I hope to share with you through these recipes.

You will encounter recipes that, because they are basic in preparation, you will find yourself using over and over again. You will also find useful resources for cooking and eating in a whole new way. However you choose to use this book, there are many dishes and flavors designed to please your sense of taste, both in eating and cooking.

Enjoy life and eat well!

Kalan Soibelman

Printed in the United States
1378600001B/88-90

9 781403 384096